Contents

D0186482

Four Comprehension Skills

Goldilocks

Retold by Chris Buckton

One fine morning, Mrs Bear made some porridge for breakfast. It was too hot to eat, so the three bears decided to go for a walk in the woods while the porridge cooled.

While they were out, a little girl called Goldilocks came running through the wood. She had lost her way. She stopped in surprise when she saw the bears' cottage. She couldn't see anybody around, so she tried the door. It opened! And when she saw the porridge on the table, she began to feel hungry…

"Nobody will notice if I just take a little bit," she thought.

In this book you will find four kinds of questions to help you to get the most out of what you are reading. Here are some examples.

Literal — **The answer's there in the text**
What did Mrs Bear make for breakfast?

Deductive — **The clues are in the text**
Why did Goldilocks go into the cottage?

Inferential — **Reading beyond the lines**
Do you think Goldilocks knew that bears lived in the cottage?

Evaluative — **Your own opinion**
Do you think Goldilocks was sensible to go into the cottage?

Judy and the Martian

by Penelope Lively

It was the middle of the night when the rocket landed in the supermarket car park. The engine had failed. The hatch opened and the Martian peered out. A Martian, I should tell you, is about three feet high and has webbed feet, green skin and eyes on the ends of horns like a snail. This one, who was three hundred and twenty-seven years old, wore a red jersey.

He said, "Bother!" He had only passed his driving test the week before, and was always losing his way. He was also an extremely nervous person, and felt the cold badly. He shivered. A car hooted and he scuttled behind a rubbish bin. Everything looked very strange and frightening.

It began to rain. He wrapped himself in a newspaper but the rain soon came through that. And then he saw that a sliding door into the back of the supermarket had been left a little bit open, just enough for him to wriggle through.

It was warmer inside, but just as frightening. There were large glass cases that hummed to themselves, and slippery floors and piles and piles of brightly coloured tins and boxes. He couldn't imagine what it was all for. He curled up between two of the humming cases and went to sleep.

30

● ● ● ●

He woke up to find everything brightly lit. He could hear people talking and walking about. He tucked himself as far out of sight as possible. Feet passed him, and silver things on wheels. Once, one with a baby in it stopped just by him. The baby leaned out and saw him and began to cry. "Ssh… !" whispered the Martian. The baby continued to shriek until its mother moved the pram on.

The Martian couldn't think what he should do. He was hungry and he wanted to go home and the bright lights and loud noises in this place made him jump. He began to cry; tears trickled down his horns. He sniffed loudly.

40

How would you feel if you landed on Mars? Does that help you understand how the Martian is feeling?

Look for words and phrases that help you work out how the Martian is feeling.

It was at this moment that a girl called Judy stopped right beside him. Her mother was hunting for fish fingers in the freezer, and Judy was pushing the trolley and also wishing she could go home: she hated shopping. She heard a peculiar fizzing noise come from the gap between the fish fingers freezer and the one beside it, and looked in.

Plenty of people looking between two freezers in a supermarket and seeing a thing there like a three-foot green snail with a red jersey on would scream. Or faint. I think I would. Not so Judy. She bent down for a closer look.

Activity

Read the story and then fill in the chart to describe the Martian's character. Give reasons for your answers.

Questions

1 Why does the rocket land in the car park?

2 Why does the Martian scuttle behind the rubbish bin?

3 When the Martian gets inside the supermarket, why is it "just as frightening"?

4 What are the humming cases?

5 Why do you think the baby who sees the Martian carries on screaming?

6 How does the the author describe the sound of the Martian sniffing?

7 What sort of girl do you think Judy is?

8 The freezer cabinets are described as "large glass cases that hummed to themselves". Choose some everyday objects and describe them from the Martian's point of view.

Inferential

The One that Got Away

Scene 3

Friday morning. The classroom

MRS COOPER • MALCOLM • MARY • DAVID • JAMES
KEVIN • WILLIAM • SARAH

Kevin: Have you got your interesting stone, Malcolm?

Malcolm: No.

Kevin: What have you got for Show and Tell, then?

Malcolm: It's a secret.

Kevin: Is it that matchbox? What's inside it?

Malcolm: Nothing. It's a secret. Go away.

10

Kevin: "Ladies and gentlemen, here is the world's most interesting matchbox!"

Mrs Cooper: Kevin, I thought you were in Class 5.

Kevin: Yes, Miss.

Mrs Cooper: Then you'd better get along there, hadn't you? Or do you want to join Class 2 today?

Kevin: No thanks, Miss.

Mrs Cooper: Come along, Class 2. Sit down and
stop talking. Have you got your
interesting things ready?

Mary: Yes, Miss. I've got my gerbil.
It's in this little cage, look.

Mrs Cooper: I think Mary had better go
first, before she bursts.

Mary: *(Holding up a little cage)* This is my gerbil.
Her name is Sally. At home
we keep her in a tank.

William: Is it full of water?

James: Does she swim?

David: She's a water gerbil!

Mary: No, the tank's got earth in it. Gerbils
live in burrows. I'm going to take her
home at dinner time so she can go back
down her hole. She used to have a
husband called Joe but she had too
many babies, so now she just lives with
another lady gerbil. That's all.

Mrs Cooper: Thank you, Mary. I should put a cloth over
Sally's cage, if I were you… Now how about
you, Malcolm? Come up here to the front.
What have you got to show us?

Malcolm: *(Holding out the matchbox)*
Here it is, Miss.

Think about how you would say these lines out loud.

Mrs Cooper: A matchbox?

Malcolm: *(Opening the matchbox)* It's in the matchbox – oh! *(He crawls about on the floor.)*

Mrs Cooper: Malcolm, what's the matter? What are you doing under the desk?

Malcolm: It's fallen out!

Mrs Cooper: What's fallen out?

Malcolm: It's a … a … it's got six legs and sharp knees and frilly ginger eyebrows on stalks.

Mary: Oh! A creepy-crawly!

Malcolm: There it goes! *(He leaps after it.)*

Mrs Cooper: Where?

Malcolm: Missed it. Hey, it's running under your chair, Mary!

Mary: *(Climbing on the table)* Eeeeeeeeh!

Mrs Cooper: Mary, get off that table. Get down.

William: I see it!

David: *(Flinging a book)* There it goes!

Mrs Cooper: David, don't throw books about.

James: *(Stamping on the floor)* I got it! I killed it!

Mary: Help, Miss. Ow, help! I felt it on my leg.

Sarah: It's crawling up the curtain.

50

60

70

William: Wooo! It's fallen in your hair, Mary.

Mary: *(Panicking)* Ah– ah– aaaaaaaah!

Mrs Cooper: Mary, be quiet. Stop screaming. There's nothing in your hair. Sit down everybody. Now, Malcolm, where's your creature?

Malcolm: I think it flew out of the window, Miss.

Mrs Cooper: I hope it did. Next time we have Show and Tell, Malcolm, you had better bring something that does not move about.

Malcolm: Yes, Miss, I'll bring my stone.

Activity

Read through the playscript again and fill in some thought bubbles for Malcolm.

Questions

1 What kind of boy do you think Malcolm is?

2 What kind of boy do you think Kevin is?

3 What do you think is in the matchbox?

4 What do you think Mary thinks is in the matchbox?

5 Do you think that Mrs Cooper believed Malcolm? Why?

6 How do you think Malcolm feels at the end of the Show and Tell session?

7 What would you bring to a Show and Tell session? Give reasons for your choice.

Inferential

SHARKS

by Chris Powling

Sharks haven't changed for millions of years. They're like leftover dinosaurs. Do sharks ever sleep? No. Do sharks ever stop swimming? No. Do sharks ever feel afraid? No.

We can say no to all these questions, at least if we're talking about the scariest shark of all. From the colour of its belly, we call this the Great White.

The Great White

When it's a thousand metres away, a Great White will hear you. When it's five hundred metres away, it'll smell you. When it's a hundred metres away, it'll notice the splash of your feet in the water. Imagine being hunted by an animal that's bigger and faster than a speedboat.

10

▼ The Great White Shark

What can you learn from the photos?

Other sorts of shark

Most sharks like the Whale Shark or the Basking Shark are more friendly.

▲ The Whale Shark

▲ The Thresher Shark

Read closely to find the facts right there in the text.

20   These are the biggest fish in the sea. Amazingly, neither will harm you. They're too busy feeding themselves. They spend hour after hour hoovering up tiny fish and plants. They won't even mind if you sneak a ride with them. A Dwarf Shark, though, could sneak a ride with you. It's the smallest shark there is.

So far, we know about more than 350 different kinds of shark. Some are so strange, they seem almost magical. It's hard to believe in the Thresher Shark.

30 The Carpet Shark, the Zebra Shark and The Goblin Shark are stranger still. And then there's the Horn Shark.

▲ The Horn Shark

Activity

PCM 5
Read *Sharks* again, and then make a list of facts about:
a) sharks in general   b) the Great White Shark

Questions

1   Why does the author call sharks like "leftover dinosaurs"?

2   What part of the Great White Shark is white?

3   What does a Basking Shark feed on?

4   How do you think the Dwarf Shark got its name?

5   How many different kinds of sharks do we know exist?

6   Which statements are true and which are false?
a) Sharks existed millions of years ago.
b) Everyone is scared of sharks.
c) Sharks are left-over dinosaurs.
d) Sharks are magical.
e) Some sharks can swim faster than speedboats.
f) A Whale Shark won't harm a human.

7   How do you think the Zebra Shark and the Carpet Shark got their names?

8   Draw a picture of what you think a Zebra Shark or a Goblin Shark might look like?

Literal

SHARK ATTACKS – *the facts*

by Cathy East Dubowski

If you're terrified of sharks, you're not alone. Shark attacks make frightening headlines, and movies like *Jaws* spread the fear that sharks are bloodthirsty killers. In fact, just the thought of sharks is enough to scare many people.

But the truth is that shark attacks are actually very rare. A person is far more likely to be hit by a car or struck by lightning than be attacked by a shark.

10

There are over 350 different species – or types – of sharks. Only about thirty of these species have ever been known to attack humans. But there are three that are really dangerous: the Great White Shark, the Bull Shark and the Tiger Shark.

▲ The Great White Shark is the most feared and fearsome of all sharks. It has even been known to attack boats.

▼ Bull Sharks are one of the few sharks that can live in both fresh and sea water.

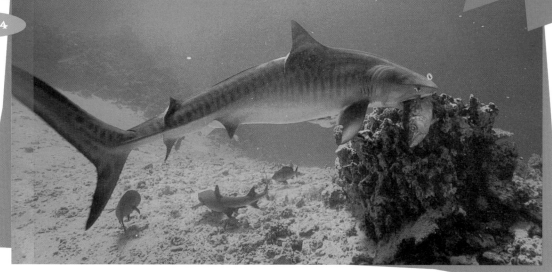

▲ A Tiger Shark is large and powerful enough to attack most sea creatures.

Divers who dive for sport or to study and film underwater life often come face to face with dangerous sharks. Some carry spear guns, or bangsticks that fire a small explosive charge that can kill a shark. But for those who want to study sharks, killing them is not the answer.

Valerie and Ron Taylor developed a new idea. These Australian film-makers are well known for their underwater photography. But it is dangerous work. Valerie has the shark bites to prove it.

On one diving trip, the Taylors noticed a crew member wearing some stainless-steel mesh gloves to protect his hands while cleaning fish. This gave them an idea. Why not make a whole diving suit out of chain-mail to protect divers from sharks – like the chain-mail suits worn by knights?

20

30

Read on to find out why "killing is not the answer".

▲ A bangstick can kill a large shark immediately.

They made a suit out of 400,000 tiny stainless-steel rings. But to test the suit, someone had to wear it in the water. Someone had to make the sharks bite!

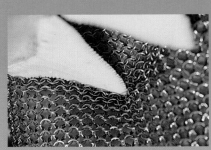

Saving their skins:
Small rings on a chain-mail suit stop a shark's teeth from biting through skin. But the diver will still be bruised.

The Taylors carried out a test dive off the coast of California. Raw chunks of fish were dumped into the water to attract sharks. Valerie Taylor zipped up the chain-mail suit over her normal diving suit, and then dived into the water among the fish chunks.

Soon, several sharks darted in. Valerie waved a bleeding fish close to her body, baiting the sharks to bite. Suddenly a shark chomped down on Valerie's arm! She was startled but not hurt.

The shark bit her again and again all over her body. It was frightening but the shark's teeth couldn't get through the mesh. The suit had worked!

▼ Valerie Taylor swimming with sharks.

But there had been some anxious moments. One shark had pulled off one of Valerie's gloves and bitten her thumb. Luckily, Valerie had managed to escape.

The suit needed small improvements. But thanks to Valerie's bravery the first practical shark suit had been invented!

60

Activity

 Read through the text on PCM 7.
a) Find the main facts and underline them.
b) Choose a fact and write it down in your own words.

Questions

1 Shark attacks are very rare. True or False?

2 How many species of sharks have been known to attack human beings?

3 What are the three most dangerous types of shark?

4 What do you think a speargun is?

5 What job do Valerie and Ron Taylor do?

6 Why do you think the crew member needed mesh gloves when he cleaned fish?

7 In order to test the diving suit, how were the sharks attracted?

8 Why was Valerie not hurt by the shark bites when she was wearing her suit?

9 What do you think is the best way to study sharks?

Literal

Aesop's Fables

retold by Malorie Blackman

The Ants and the Grasshopper

It was summer. And while the ants gathered seeds and nuts for the cold days to come, Grasshopper jumped about and sang happily in the sun. But summer didn't last forever. Winter came. It blew cold and hard and fierce. Poor Grasshopper was starving. There was no food anywhere. Dying of hunger and cold he made his way to the ants and begged them for something to eat.

10   "And what were you doing in summer while we were working hard to gather up all this food?" the ants asked.

"I was singing," the grasshopper replied.

"Really!" said the ants, less than impressed. "Well, as you sang then, you can dance now – and see where that gets you."

Moral: A smart person puts something away for when times are bad.

What is the most important thing to learn from this fable?

The Sun and the North Wind

"When you get right down to it, I'm stronger than you," said the North Wind.

"You really think so?" smiled the Sun.

"All right then, I'll prove it," said the North Wind. "You see that man down there with a coat on? I bet I can blow his coat right off. Watch this!"

And the North Wind blew and blew and blew. He blew around the man's head, around his legs, around his back and his chest, trying to tear his coat off.

10 But the man just pulled his coat even more firmly around him, shivering against the cold.

"D'you mind if I have a try?" said the Sun.

And he shone. Warm, soft, golden rays.

"What funny peculiar weather!" said the man, unbuttoning his coat.

And the Sun shone some more. Bright, light rays everywhere.

"I'm melting," the man gasped. And he pulled off his coat and
20 slung it over his shoulder.

"I win! I win!" grinned the Sun. "Deal with that!"

Moral: Persuasion works better than force.

Activity

PCM 9 Read "The Sun and the North Wind" and then match each paragraph to the main idea it fits best.

Questions

The Ants and the Grasshopper

1 Which *one* word best describes the Grasshopper?
a) foolish   b) lazy   c) happy

2 Why did the Grasshopper have no food in winter?

3 Why do you think the Grasshopper does not store food?

The Sun and the North Wind

4 Find all the words or phrases that tell us the Wind is very forceful and all the words or phrases that tell us the Sun is gentle. Put them in two columns.

5 Which worked better, the North Wind's force, or the Sun's persuasion? How do you know?

6 Why is it important that we still read these stories today?

Deductive

A Lion in the Meadow

by Margaret Mahy

The little boy said,

"Mother, there is a lion in the meadow."

The mother said,

"Nonsense, little boy."

The little boy said,

"Mother, there is a big yellow lion in the meadow."

The mother said,

"Nonsense, little boy."

The little boy said,

"Mother there is a big, roaring, yellow, whiskery lion in the meadow!"

The mother said,

"Little boy, you are making up stories again. There is nothing in the meadow but grass and trees. Go into the meadow and see for yourself."

The little boy said,

"Mother, I'm scared to go into the meadow because of the lion which is there."

What is the most important sentence on the page?

10

20   The mother said,

    "Little boy, you are making up stories – so I will make up a story, too… Do you see this match box? Take it out into the meadow and open it. In it will be a tiny dragon. The tiny dragon will grow into a big dragon. It will chase the lion away."

    The little boy took the match box and went away. The mother went on peeling the potatoes.

    Suddenly the door opened.

    In rushed a big, roaring, yellow, whiskery lion.

    "Hide me!" it said. "A dragon is after me."

30   The lion hid in the broom cupboard.

    Then the little boy came running in.

    "Mother," he said, "that dragon grew too big. There is no lion in the meadow now. There is a DRAGON in the meadow."

    The little boy hid in the broom cupboard too.

    "You should have left me alone," said the lion. "I eat only apples."

"But there wasn't a real dragon," said the
40 mother. "It was just a story I made up."

"It turned out to be true after all," said the little
boy. "You should have looked in the match box first."

"That is how it is," said the lion. "Some stories are
true and some aren't…

"But I have an idea. We will go and play in the
meadow on the other side of the house. There is no
dragon there."

"I am glad we are friends now," said the little boy.

The little boy and the big, roaring, yellow,
50 whiskery lion went to play in the other meadow. The
dragon stayed where he was, and nobody minded.

The mother never, ever, made up a story again.

Activity

 Read the story again, and then choose the lesson that fits the story best, giving reasons. Why do you think the mother "never, ever, made up a story again"?

Questions

1. What does the word "meadow" mean?
   a) a field   b) a farmyard   c) a wood

2. How do you know if the mother believes the little boy or not?

3. Why do you think the mother chooses a dragon to be in the matchbox?

4. Think of three things that are unusual about the lion in the story.

5. Why do you think the lion says that he eats only apples?

6. Why doesn't the mother believe the little boy?

7. Who has a lesson to learn? Write, in one sentence, what it might be.

In this fable, the main idea appears in the last sentence.

Deductive

HAIRCUT RAP

by Valerie Bloom

Tap out the beat as you read. Does it work?

Ah sey, ah want it short,
Short back an' side,
Ah tell him, man, ah tell him
When ah teck him aside,
Ah sey, ah want a haircut
Ah can wear with pride,
So lef' it long on top
But short back an' side.

Ah sey try an' put a pattern
In the shorter part,
Yuh could put a skull an' crossbone,
Or an arrow through a heart.
Meck sure ah have enough hair lef'
Fe cover me wart,
Lef a likkle pon the top,
But the res' – keep it short.

Well, bwoy, him start to cut
An' me settle down to wait.
Him was cuttin' from seven
Till half-past eight.
Ah was startin' to get worried
'Cause ah see it gettin' late,
But then him put the scissors down,
Sey, "There yuh are, mate."

Well, ah did see a skull an' a
Criss-cross bone or two,
But was me own skull an' bone
That was peepin' through.
Ah look jus' like a monkey
30 Ah did see once at the zoo,
Him say, "What's de matter, Tammy,
Don't yuh like the hair-do?"

Well, ah feel me heart stop beatin'
When me look pon me reflection,
Ah feel like somet'ing frizzle up
Right in me middle section.
Ah look aroun' fe somewhey
Ah could crawl an' hide,
The day I meck me brother cut
40 Me hair short back an' side.

Re-read the poem aloud. Does it sound better?

Activity

PCM 13 Read through the poem with a partner. Fill in the chart to say how you felt about it.

Questions

1 How long did the haircut take?

2 How short did his brother cut his hair, and how do you know?

3 Which line tells you how Tammy felt about his new haircut?

4 What does Tammy want to do afterwards?

5 Which part of the poem do you like best? Give reasons for your answers.

6 Did you find it easier to read the poem quietly or out loud?

7 Do you think this is a good performance poem? Explain your answer.

Evaluative

Colour Waves
by Neil Buchanan

Here's a sort of 3-D wave that plays tricks on your eyes. To make it really effective, stick it on to a piece of contrasting backing card.

From paper to 3-D pattern

1. Take a sheet of white paper and draw a criss-cross pattern of wavy lines. Place a wobbly cross inside each square.

Materials

Backing card
White paper
Coloured pencils
Scissors
Glue stick
Marker pen

Roll back the edges of the shorter sides of the wavy pattern to create 3-D curls.

Colouring tip

First put a small dot of the right colour in each of the triangles so that you don't go wrong.

Leave the top triangle white.

10   **2.** Colour the squares using black in the bottom triangle and two shades of the same colour for the left and right.

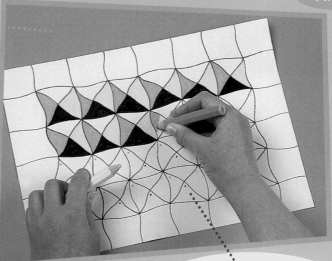

Only colour in the squares that do not border the edge of the paper.

3. It is important to colour each square in exactly the same way to make the picture really effective. When you 20 have finished, cut out the coloured pattern.

4. Stick your pattern on to a piece of contrasting backing. Complete the 3-D wave by pushing the edges of the sheet of paper inwards from both sides.

It's important to have a bright colour as the background so that the waves really show up.

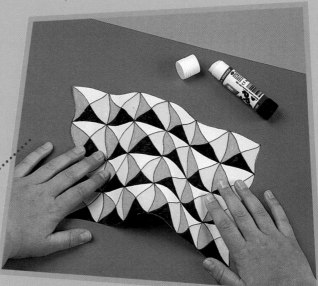

Folding frenzy

30 Try experimenting with the paper folds by making them as big or small as you like. Why not have a really big fold at the top and a small one at the bottom?

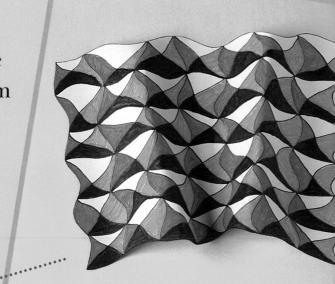

Put your picture on the wall and impress your friends with your weird, wavy pattern.

Wave variations

Make lots of your own wavy patterns, but remember to keep to the same colour theme on each one. For the most effective look, use black, white and two
40 shades of the same colour. Have fun making waves!

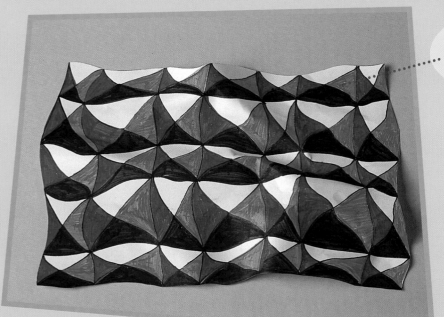

The more squares you draw, the more wavy your picture will be.

Think about what makes these instructions easy to follow.

Waves of colour

The more you bend the paper into waves, the more effective your wavy pattern will look. Glue the underside of the paper between each wave so that the waves really stand up. Hang your picture on a wall and admire your very own 3-D wavy pattern.

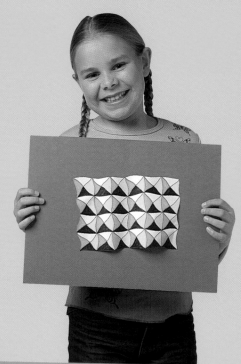

Activity

 PCM 15 Read through "Colour Waves" again with a partner and fill in the chart to say whether the instructions were clear.

Questions

1 What tip does the author give to help you avoid colouring the wrong triangle?

2 Would a red and yellow colour wave be as effective as a pink and red colour wave? Find the sentence that tells us.

3 What do you need the marker pen for?

4 If you were going to make Colour Waves, which text feature would help you most?

5 What would be the best way to find out how well the instructions work?

Evaluative

The Magpie Song

by Laurence Anholt

Carla and her parents have moved to the city.
Carla keeps in touch with her Grandad through letters.

Dear Grandad,
I don't like it much at school. I can't do anything right. Today, Mum was late to collect me and Mrs Evans was cross.

It was really cold waiting for the bus. It began to snow, but it didn't make the ground all white – just muddy and grey.

At home the lift wasn't working, and we had to carry the shopping up all 574 steps to the flat. When we got in, Dad had already gone to work.

Did it snow where you are? Are there any wild animals in the woods?

Love from
Carla

Think about your first day at school. What was it like?

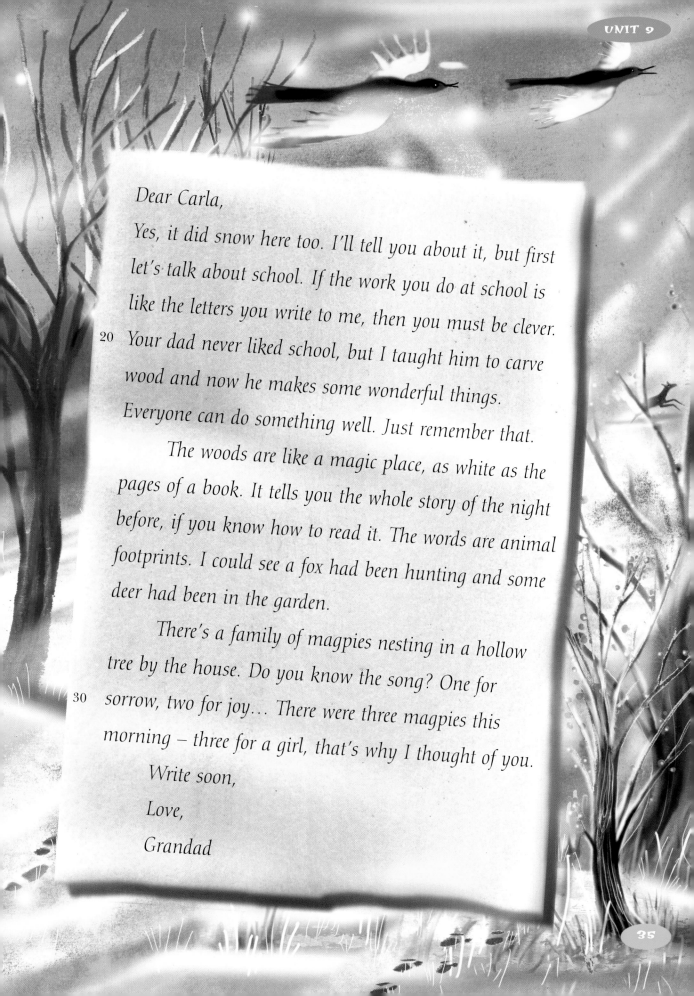

Dear Carla,

Yes, it did snow here too. I'll tell you about it, but first let's talk about school. If the work you do at school is like the letters you write to me, then you must be clever.

20 Your dad never liked school, but I taught him to carve wood and now he makes some wonderful things. Everyone can do something well. Just remember that.

The woods are like a magic place, as white as the pages of a book. It tells you the whole story of the night before, if you know how to read it. The words are animal footprints. I could see a fox had been hunting and some deer had been in the garden.

There's a family of magpies nesting in a hollow tree by the house. Do you know the song? One for 30 sorrow, two for joy… There were three magpies this morning – three for a girl, that's why I thought of you.

Write soon,

Love,

Grandad

Activity

PCM 17 Read Grandad's reply again, and write down what he says in each paragraph in just a few words.

Questions

1 Why do you think Carla's mum is late to collect her?

2 What happens when Mum is late?

3 Why do you think Carla's dad leaves for work when she gets home?

4 Why do you think Grandad tells Carla that her dad carves beautiful things?

5 Why does Grandad say the woods are like a magic place?

6 How can Grandad read "the story of the night before" in the snow?

Inferential

Amina's Blanket

by Helen Dunmore

A crash like a thousand storms ripped through the building. It picked up Josie and Amina and threw them across the room. There was a terrible rumbling as if the building were falling apart, and the starlit sky showed where the window had once been. Josie's mouth was full of dust and smoke. She coughed and choked. The blanket was gone, Amina was gone, Sinta was gone. She could smell burning. How close was it? Was it in the building?

● ● ● ●

10   "Amina!" Josie whispered. She couldn't shout because of all the dust.

"Josie!" came a little croaky voice from under the window.

"What happened? Did something hit us?"

Which senses do the images appeal to?

"It was close. The closest we've had."

"Is there a fire?"

The light in the window was changing to red.
Amina got up and peered out. "There's a fire just
down the street," she told Josie. Josie picked herself
20 up off the floor and stumbled over to Amina. She saw
long red flames licking out of a block of flats, and
people, like black ants, running in the streets. Fire
leapt into the sky, changing it from dark blue to
orange. It was nearly as light as day.

"Poor Sinta," said Amina. "He's so frightened of
shells. He's afraid we'll get hit."

"Where is he?"

"In my pocket, right down at the bottom. Can you
feel him?" Josie felt the little shivering mouse, deep
30 in Amina's pocket. The walls of Amina's
room were shivering too.

"The fire is spreading," said Amina. "It's coming this way. I wish Mum was here."

The fire crackled and rushed. It sounded as if it was nearly in the room. Then Josie and Amina heard voices shouting. The voices were coming nearer and nearer.

"Rescuers!" said Amina. "They're coming to get us out!"

The fire was coming closer. Which would get to them first, the fire or the rescuers? Josie grabbed Amina's hand, and they stumbled to the broken doorway. There was so much smoke that their eyes hurt. Josie coughed when she tried to breathe, and the fire roared like a lion outside. Suddenly the rescuers' voices were loud, just on the other side of the door.

"We're in here!" shouted Amina.

40

Have you ever been scared?

Activity

PCM 19 Work with a partner to pick out words that describe the look, sound, touch, taste and smell of the explosion. Write on the chart or draw a picture to show what it was like.

Questions

1 Why is the light in the window "changing to red"?

2 Why do you think the author describes the flames as "licking"?

3 Why are the people described as "black ants"?

4 Who is Sinta?

5 Why are the mouse and the walls "shivering"?
Is it for the same reason?

6 Why do you think Amina wishes her mother was there?

7 How do you think the girls will escape?

8 Describe a frightening event, such as a fire. Think about all the senses that might be affected.

Inferential

Eddie and the Bad Egg

by Herbie Brennan

CHAPTER 1:

Chicken in the soup

My name is Eddie. I'm a duck.
I run a downtown ducktective
agency.

It was a slow day at the office.
But then there was a knock on
my door.

"Come in," I called. That's
what I do when somebody knocks.

The door opened. My girl,
Gloria, brought in a frozen
chicken.

"Who's this?" I asked.

"Don't you recognise your
cousin Charlie?" growled the
chicken.

I took off my shades so
I could see him better.
"Charlie? Charlie Chicken?
You look awful."

10

20   "I'm just cold," Charlie shrugged. "What happened to the heat in here?"

"Got cut off when I didn't pay the bill," I told him.

"All ducks have bills," said Charlie sympathetically.

I hauled my feet off the desk and waddled over to the filing cabinet. I found a bottle under B and poured us both a shot of

30 swamp water.

"What brings you into town?" I asked.

"It's my boy Larry," Charlie said. "He's got himself mixed up with a bunch of gangsters."

It didn't surprise me. Even as a youngster, Larry was a bad egg. But I said nothing.

What does it mean to be a "bad egg"? Try reading what Charlie said to work it out.

40 Charlie sipped his swamp water. "They're planning to smuggle in some lowlife from South America. Small-time criminal calls himself Mr Big. If Larry gets caught, they'll lock him in a coop and throw away the key."

I sniffed, which is hard to do when you're a duck. "What do you want me to do about it?"

Charlie looked me straight in my beady eye. "Catch the gangsters," he said sourly. "And talk some sense into my boy Larry."

Activity

PCM
21

Read "Eddie and the Bad Egg" again. Find where the author has used puns or words that play with language and work out what they mean.

Questions

1 Who is telling the story?

2 Do you think Eddie is good at his job?

3 Why is the swamp-water filed under B?

4 Who is the "bad egg"?

5 What does "coop" usually mean and what does it mean here?

6 Why is the criminal called Mr Big?

7 Why do you think this chapter is called "Chicken in the Soup"?

Deductive

Spells

by James Reeves

I dance and dance without any feet –
This is the spell of the ripening wheat.

With never a tongue I've a tale to tell –
This is the meadow-grasses' spell.

I give you health without any fee –
This is the spell of the apple tree.

I rhyme and riddle without any book –
This is the spell of the bubbling brook.

Without any legs I run for ever –
This is the spell of the mighty river.

I fall for ever and not at all –
This is the spell of the waterfall.

10

Without a voice I roar aloud –
This is the spell of the thunder-cloud.

No button or seam has my white coat –
This is the spell of the leaping goat.

I can cheat strangers with never a word –
This is the spell of the cuckoo-bird.

We have tongues in plenty but speak no names
20   This is the spell of the fiery flames.

The creaking door has a spell to riddle –
I play a tune without any fiddle.

Did you work out what the riddles meant before you read the answers? What clues did the poet give?

Activity

PCM 23 Explain some of the riddles in the rest of the poem. Choose one that you like and draw a picture of it.

Questions

1 Why does the coat of the goat have no button or seam?

2 What tale might the meadow-grass tell you?

3 Why does a field of wheat's movement bring dancing to mind?

4 Why does the poet describe the flames as "tongues"?

5 Which of the following might give you health without a fee?
a) fresh air   b) orange juice
c) a long walk   d) vitamin pills

6 Why is this poem called "Spells"?

Deductive

Series Author: Catherine Byrne
Series Consultant: Chris Buckton

Heinemann
Halley Court, Jordan Hill, Oxford, OX2 8EJ
a division of Reed Educational and Professional Publishing Ltd
www.heinemann.co.uk

Heinemann is a registered trademark of Reed Educational and Professional Publishing Ltd

©Reed Educational and Professional Publishing Ltd 2002

Total Comprehension Anthology for Year 3

ISBN 0435 16341 8 (single copy)
ISBN 0435 16345 0 (6-pack)

06 05 04 03 02
10 9 8 7 6 5 4 3 2 1

Designed by Alicia Howard at Tangerine Tiger
Origination by EPC Direct : UK
Printed in Scotland by Scotprint

Acknowledgements

The publisher would like to thank the following for permission to reproduce extracts from their copyright material:

INTRODUCTION **Goldilocks** by Chris Buckton. Illustrated by John Haslam.

UNIT 1 **Judy and the Martian** by Penelope Lively, published by Macdonald Young Books, 1992. Reproduced by permission of Hodder and Stoughton Limited. Illustrated by Jenny Grahame/Beehive Illustration.

UNIT 2 **The One That Got Away** © Jan Mark, 1994, from Reading 360 Plays published by Ginn. Reproduced by permission of David Higham Associates Limited. Illustrated by Bridget MacKeith.

UNIT 3 **Sharks** by Chris Powling, published by Oxford University Press, 2000. Reproduced by permission of David Higham Associates Limited. **Photos:** Great White Shark: Ant photo library/NHPA. Whale Shark: NHPA. Thresher Shark: Scott Tuason/imagequest 3d.com; group of Hammerhead Sharks: Ant photo library/NHPA. Horn Shark: Richard Herrmann/Oxford Scientific Films.

UNIT 4 **Shark Attacks** © the facts Cathy East Dubowski, 1998, published by Dorling Kindersley. Reproduced by permission of the publisher.
Photos: Great White shark: Mark Bowler/NHPA; Other photographs: Ron and Valerie Taylor/Ardea London Ltd.

UNIT 5 **Aesop's Fables** retold by Malorie Blackman, published by Scholastic, 1998. Reproduced by permission of the publisher. Illustrated by Phil Garner/Beehive Illustration.

UNIT 6 **A Lion in the Meadow** by Margaret Mahy from *The Little Witch* published by Orion Children's Books. Reproduced by permission of the publisher. Illustrated by Emma Chichester Clark.

UNIT 7 **"Haircut Rap"** © Valerie Bloom, from *The Works* published by Macmillan, 2000. Reproduced by kind permission of the author. Illustrated by Lydia Monks.

UNIT 8 **Colour Waves** © Neil Buchanan,1999, published by Dorling Kindersley. Reproduced by permission of The Penguin Group (UK). Demonstrator: Emily Howard. Photos: John Williams.

UNIT 9 **The Magpie Song** by Laurence Anholt, published by Mammoth, 1995. © Egmont Children's Books. Illustrated by Bee Willey.

UNIT 10 **Amina's Blanket** by Helen Dunmore, published by Heinemann Young Books, 1996. © Egmont Children's Books. Illustrated by Alan Marks.

UNIT 11 **Eddie and the Bad Egg** © Herbie Brennan, 2000, published by Puffin. Reproduced by permission of The Penguin Group (UK) and Ed Victor Limited. Illustrated by Andy Hammond.

UNIT 12 **"Spells"** © James Reeves from *Complete Poems for Children* published by Heinemann. Reproduced by permission of Laura Cecil Literary Agency on behalf of the James Reeves Estate. Illustrated by Bee Willey.

Cover Illustration by Louise Ellis/The Organisation